A LONG OBEDIENCE

EUGENE H. PETERSON

IN THE SAME

DIRECTION

DISCIPLESHIP IN AN INSTANT SOCIETY

6 STUDIES FOR INDIVIDUALS OR GROUPS

ivp
Bible
Studies

An imprint of InterVarsity Press
Downers Grove, Illinois

InterVarsity Press
P.O. Box 1400 | Downers Grove, IL 60515-1426
ivpress.com | email@ivpress.com

This study guide is based on and adapts material from *A Long Obedience in the Same Direction* ©1980 by InterVarsity Christian Fellowship of the United States of America.

Originally published as *Perseverance: A Long Obedience in the Same Direction*. Published in this format in 2021.

InterVarsity Press® is the publishing division of InterVarsity Christian Fellowship/USA®. For more information, visit intervarsity.org.

All Scripture quotations, unless otherwise indicated, are taken from The Holy Bible, New International Version®, NIV®. Copyright © 1973, 1978, 1984, 2011 by Biblica, Inc.™ Used by permission of Zondervan. All rights reserved worldwide. www.zondervan.com. The "NIV" and "New International Version" are trademarks registered in the United States Patent and Trademark Office by Biblica, Inc.™

Cover design: Kate Lillard
Interior design: Daniel van Loon
Image: Mountain landscape photo © Kalen Emsley / unsplash.com

ISBN 978-1-5140-1305-2 (print) | ISBN 978-0-8308-5073-0 (digital)

Printed in the United States of America ♾

32   31   30   29   28   27   26   25 | 13   12   11   10   9   8   7   6   5   4   3   2

CONTENTS

GETTING
THE MOST OUT OF

A LONG OBEDIENCE IN THE SAME DIRECTION BIBLE STUDY

Knowing Christ is where faith begins. From there we are shaped through the essentials of discipleship: Bible study, prayer, Christian community, worship, and much more. We learn to grow in Christlike character, pursue justice, and share our faith with others. We persevere through doubts and gain wisdom for daily life. These are the topics woven into the IVP Signature Bible Studies. Working through this series will help you practice the essentials by exploring biblical truths found in classic books.

HOW IT'S PUT TOGETHER

Each session includes an opening quotation and suggested reading from the book *A Long Obedience in the Same Direction*, a session goal to help guide your study, reflection questions to stir your thoughts on the topic, the text of the Bible passage, questions for exploring the passage, response questions to help you apply what you've learned, and a closing suggestion for prayer.

The workbook format is ideal for personal study and also allows group members to prepare in advance for discussions and record discussion notes. The responses you write here can form a permanent record of your thoughts and spiritual progress.

Throughout the guide are study-note sidebars that may be useful for group leaders or individuals. These notes do not give the answers, but they do provide additional background information on certain questions and can challenge participants to think deeper or differently about the content.

WHAT KIND OF GUIDE IS THIS?

The studies are not designed to merely tell you what one person thinks. Instead, through inductive study, they will help you discover for yourself what Scripture is saying. Each study deals with a particular passage—rather than jumping around the Bible—so that you can really delve into the biblical author's meaning in that context.

The studies ask three different kinds of questions about the Bible passage:

- *Observation* questions help you to understand the content of the passage by asking about the basic facts: who, what, when, where, and how.

- *Interpretation* questions delve into the meaning of the passage.

- *Application* questions help you discover implications for growing in Christ in your own life.

These three keys unlock the treasures of the biblical writings and help you live them out.

This is a thought-provoking guide. Each question assumes a variety of answers. Many questions do not have "right" answers, particularly questions that aim at meaning or application. Instead, the questions should inspire readers to explore the passage more thoroughly.

This study guide is flexible. You can use it for individual study, but it is also great for a variety of groups—student, professional, neighborhood, or church groups. Each study takes about forty-five minutes in a group setting or thirty minutes in personal study.

SUGGESTIONS FOR INDIVIDUAL STUDY

1. This guide is based on a classic book that will enrich your spiritual life. If you have not read *A Long Obedience in the Same Direction*, you may want to read the portion recommended in the "Read" section before you begin your study. The ideas in the book will enhance your study, but the Bible text will be the focus of each session.

2. Begin each session with prayer, asking God to speak to you from his Word about this particular topic.

3. As you read the Scripture passage, reproduced for you from the New International Version, you may wish to mark phrases that seem important. Note in the margin any questions that come to your mind.

4. Close with the suggested prayer found at the end of each session. Speak to God about insights you have gained. Tell him of any desires you have for specific growth. Ask him to help you attempt to live out the principles described in that passage. You may wish to write your own prayer in this guide or a journal.

SUGGESTIONS FOR GROUP MEMBERS

Joining a Bible study group can be a great avenue to spiritual growth. Here are a few guidelines that will help you as you participate in the studies in this guide.

1. Reading the recommended portion of *A Long Obedience in the Same Direction*, before or after each session, will enhance your study and understanding of the themes in this guide.

2. These studies use methods of inductive Bible study, which focuses on a particular passage of Scripture and works on it in depth. So try to dive into the given text instead of referring to other Scripture passages.

3. Questions are designed to help a group discuss together a passage of Scripture in order to understand its content, meaning, and implications. Most people are either natural talkers or natural listeners, yet this type of study works best if all members participate more or less evenly. Try to curb any natural tendency toward either excessive talking or excessive quiet. You and the rest of the group will benefit!

4. Most questions in this guide allow for a variety of answers. If you disagree with someone else's comment, gently say so. Then explain your own point of view from the passage before you.

5. Be willing to lead a discussion, if asked. Much of the preparation for leading has already been accomplished in the writing of this guide.

6. Respect the privacy of people in your group. Many people share things within the context of a Bible study group that they do not want to be public knowledge. Assume that personal information spoken within the group setting is private, unless you are specifically told otherwise.

7. We recommend that all groups agree on a few basic guidelines. You may wish to adapt this list to your situation:

   a. Anything said in this group is considered confidential and will not be discussed outside the group unless specific permission is given to do so.

   b. We will provide time for each person present to talk if he or she feels comfortable doing so.

   c. We will talk about ourselves and our own situations, avoiding conversation about other people.

   d. We will listen attentively to each other.

   e. We will pray for each other.

8. Enjoy your study. Prepare to grow!

SUGGESTIONS FOR GROUP LEADERS

There are specific suggestions to help you in the "Leading a Small Group" section. It describes how to lead a group discussion, gives helpful tips on group dynamics, and suggests ways to deal with problems that may arise during the discussion. With such helps, someone with little or no experience can lead an effective group study. Read this section carefully, even if you are leading only one group meeting.

TOURISTS
AND PILGRIMS

*The essential thing "in heaven and earth" is . . . that there should be long
obedience in the same direction; there thereby results, and has always
resulted in the long run, something which has made life worth living.*

FRIEDRICH NIETZSCHE, *BEYOND GOOD AND EVIL*

This world is no friend to grace. When a person makes a commitment to Jesus Christ as Lord and Savior, a crowd does not immediately form to applaud the decision, nor do old friends spontaneously gather around to offer congratulations and counsel. Ordinarily there are no directly hostile reactions; nevertheless, others' puzzled disapproval and agnostic indifference make surprisingly formidable opposition.

It is nearly as hard for a sinner to recognize the world's temptations as it is for a fish to discover impurities in the water. There is a sense that things aren't right, that the environment is not whole, but just what the problem is eludes analysis. We know that the spiritual atmosphere in which we live erodes faith, dissipates hope, and corrupts love; but it is hard to put our finger on what is wrong.

THE LURE OF INSTANT RESULTS

One aspect of this world that I have been able to identify as harmful to Christians is the assumption that anything worthwhile can be acquired at once. We assume that if something can be done at all, it can be done quickly and efficiently. Our attention spans have been conditioned by thirty-second commercials. Our sense of reality has been flattened by thirty-page abridgments.

In our culture anything, even news about God, can be sold if it is packaged freshly; but when it loses its novelty, it goes on the garbage heap. There is a great market for religious experience in our world; there is little enthusiasm for the patient acquisition of virtue, little inclination to sign up for a long apprenticeship in what earlier generations of Christians called *holiness*.

The persons whom I lead in worship, among whom I counsel, visit, pray, preach, and teach, want shortcuts. They want me to help them fill out the form that will get them instant credit (in eternity). They are impatient for results. They have adopted the lifestyle of a tourist and want only the high points. But a pastor is not a tour guide. I have no interest in telling apocryphal religious stories at and around dubiously identified sacred sites. The Christian life cannot mature under such conditions and in such ways.

A DOG-EARED SONGBOOK

In the pastoral work of training people in discipleship and accompanying them in pilgrimage, I have found, tucked away in the Hebrew Psalter, an old, dog-eared songbook. I have used it to provide continuity in guiding others in the Christian way and directing people of faith in the conscious and continuous effort that develops into maturity in Christ. The songs are the psalms numbered 120 through 134 in the book of Psalms.

These fifteen psalms were likely sung, possibly in sequence, by Hebrew pilgrims as they went up to Jerusalem to the great worship festivals. Jerusalem was the highest city geographically in Palestine, and so all who traveled there spent much of their time ascending.

But the ascent was not only literal, it was also metaphorical: the trip to Jerusalem acted out a life lived upward toward God, an existence that advanced from one level to another in developing maturity. It's what Paul described as "the upward call of God in Christ Jesus" (Philippians 3:14 RSV).

This picture of the Hebrews singing these fifteen psalms as they left their routines of discipleship and made their way from towns and villages, farms and cities, as pilgrims up to Jerusalem has become embedded in the Christian devotional imagination. It is our best background for understanding life as a faith journey. There are no better "songs for the road" for those who travel the way of faith in Christ.

For those who choose to live no longer as tourists, but as pilgrims, the Psalms of Ascents combine all the cheerfulness of a travel song with the practicality of a guidebook and map. Their unpretentious brevity is excellently described by William Faulkner: "They are not monuments, but footprints. A monument only says, 'At least I got this far,' while a footprint says, 'This is where I was when I moved again.'"*

---

*William Faulkner, quoted in Sam di Bonaventura's Program Notes to Elie Siegmeister's Symphony No. 5, Baltimore Symphony Concert, May 5, 1977.

REPENTANCE

PSALM 120

My grandfather left Norway over a century ago in the midst of a famine. His wife and ten children remained behind until he could return and get them. He came to Pittsburgh and worked in the steel mills for two years until he had enough money to go back and get his family. When he returned with them, he didn't stay in Pittsburgh, although it had served his purposes well enough the first time. Instead he traveled on to Montana, plunging into new land, looking for a better place.

In all immigrant stories there are mixed parts of escape and adventure: the escape from an unpleasant situation and the adventure of a far better way of life, free for new things, open for growth and creativity. Every Christian can tell some variation on this immigrant plot.

"Woe to me that I dwell in Meshek, that I live among the tents of Kedar! Too long have I lived among those who hate peace." This is the text of Psalm 120. But we don't have to live there any longer. Repentance, the first word in Christian immigration, sets us on the way to traveling in the light. It is a rejection that is also an acceptance, a leaving that develops into an arriving, a *no* to the world that is a *yes* to God.

SESSION GOAL	READ
Encourage us to turn from sin and toward the Lord.	Chapters one through three of *A Long Obedience in the Same Direction*

REFLECT

○ What aspects of your own world do you find distressing or unsatisfying?

○ What motivates you to turn away from sin and move toward greater closeness with God?

STUDY

READ PSALM 120.

[1]I call on the LORD in my distress,
   and he answers me.
[2]Save me, LORD,
   from lying lips
   and from deceitful tongues.
[3]What will he do to you,
   and what more besides,
   you deceitful tongue?
[4]He will punish you with a warrior's sharp arrows,
   with burning coals of the broom bush.

⁵Woe to me that I dwell in Meshek,
 that I live among the tents of Kedar!
⁶Too long have I lived
 among those who hate peace.
⁷I am for peace;
 but when I speak, they are for war.

1. Throughout this passage, what words and phrases reveal how the writer feels about his society?

2. As the psalmist begins the ascent toward God's temple in Jerusalem, what does he feel distressed about (vv. 1-2)?

"The psalms are full of references to the sins of the tongue—lies, scandal, slander, hypocrisy." People of God "may suffer as much from what people say as from what they do."*

3. What does the psalmist ask the Lord to do for him in his distress?

4. Note the strong imagery of the punishments in verse 4. Why do you think the deceitful tongue deserves such harsh punishment?

It is good to remember that the "deceitful tongue" of verse 3 could be the writer's own—or ours! We are called to reject sin no matter where we find it, in others or in ourselves.

5. How are your own feelings about sin like or unlike what the psalmist expresses?

6. How does the sin the psalmist identifies in verses 6-7 compare or contrast with the sin in verses 1-2?

7. Sometimes sins that are rooted deep in our culture are difficult to identify—and may take root in us. How has this been true for you?

The first step toward God is a step away from the lies of the world. It is a renunciation of the lies we have been told about ourselves and our neighbors and our universe. Repentance is not an emotion. It is not feeling sorry for your sins. It is a decision. It is deciding you have been wrong in supposing that you could manage your own life and be your own god; it is deciding that you were wrong in thinking that you had, or could get, the strength, education, and training to make it on your own.

8. How does the psalmist think and act decisively about sin?

RESPOND

○ What undesirable elements in your environment do you need to move away from—without breaking godly commitments?

○ How can you take that step?

○ While we cannot always move away from worldliness, we can always repent and abandon it in our hearts. What sin(s) do you need to confess and forsake?

Search your own heart and repent of any sins of worldliness. Prayer-
fully take the step of moving away from the world and toward God.
Begin—or renew—your commitment to be a pilgrim.

---

*David Alexander and Pat Alexander, eds., *Eerdmans' Handbook to the Bible* (Grand Rapids,
MI: Eerdmans, 1973), 350.

HELP

PSALM 124

I was at a Red Cross bloodmobile to donate my annual pint. A nurse asked me a series of questions to see if there was any reason for disqualification. The final question on the list was, "Do you engage in hazardous work?" I said, "Yes."

She looked up, a little surprised, for I was wearing a clerical collar by which she could identify me as a pastor. Her hesitation was only momentary; she smiled, ignored my answer, and marked the "no" on her questionnaire, saying, "I don't mean *that* kind of hazardous."

I would have liked to continue the conversation, comparing what she supposed I meant by hazardous with what I meant by it. But that was not the appropriate time and place. A line of people was waiting for their turn at the needle. There are, though, appropriate times and places for just such conversations, and one of them is when Christians encounter Psalm 124. Psalm 124 is a song of hazard—and of help. Among the Psalms of Ascents sung by the people of God on the way of faith, this is one that, better than any other, describes the hazardous work of discipleship and declares the help that is always experienced at the hand of God.

SESSION GOAL	**READ**
Praise God for his help in the past and trust him for future deliverance.	Chapters four through six of *A Long Obedience in the Same Direction*

REFLECT

○ When have you survived danger, either physical or spiritual, through the Lord's help?

○ When or how do you feel the Lord has not helped or rescued you? What do you wish God had done in those cases?

STUDY

READ PSALM 124.

¹If the LORD had not been on our side—
    let Israel say—
²if the LORD had not been on our side
    when people attacked us,
³they would have swallowed us alive
    when their anger flared against us;
⁴the flood would have engulfed us,
    the torrent would have swept over us,
⁵the raging waters
    would have swept us away.

⁶Praise be to the LORD,
   who has not let us be torn by their teeth.
⁷We have escaped like a bird
   from the fowler's snare;
the snare has been broken,
   and we have escaped.
⁸Our help is in the name of the LORD,
   the Maker of heaven and earth.

1. The psalmist and all God's people had been under vicious attack. What words depict the strength of the attack they had to endure?

The people were in danger of being swallowed up alive and drowned. The first picture is of an enormous dragon or sea monster. The second, that of a flood, is a picture of sudden disaster. In the Middle East, watercourses that have eroded the countryside are all interconnected by an intricate, gravitational system. A sudden storm fills the little gullies with water, they feed into one another, and in a few minutes a torrential flash flood is produced. People who live in these desert areas are endangered during the rainy season by such unannounced catastrophes.

2. What would have been their destiny if God had not rescued them (vv. 3-6)?

> The psalmist is not talking about the good life, how God
> has kept him out of all difficulty. This person has gone
> through the worst—the dragon's mouth, the flood's
> torrent—and finds himself intact. He was not abandoned
> but helped. The final strength is not in the dragon or in
> the flood but in "the LORD" who was "on our side."

3. Gnashing teeth, raging floods, and treacherous snares were part
   of the psalmist's reality. How are they part of the reality you are
   facing now? (They may take the form of persecutions, temptations, physical problems, conflicts, or anything else that
   threatens your faith.)

4. To what does the psalmist compare their escape (v. 7)?

> The image of danger changes from floodwaters to "the
> fowler's snare," which also occurs in Psalm 91:3. This bird
> trap "consisted of a roughly circular wooden base on which
> two nets were mounted. When the trap was set, the nets
> were drawn down to one side and held in place by a trigger,
> which, when released, allowed the nets to spring up and
> envelop the victim. The trigger could be released by hand,
> or sprung when the victim touched the bait attached to it."*

5. When and how has the Lord helped you persevere in dangerous times?

6. How does your history with the Lord give you hope that he will deliver you safely through danger?

7. The last verse of the psalm proclaims that "our help is in the name of the Lord, the Maker of heaven and earth." How is your trust in God affected by the knowledge that he is the Creator of all?

RESPOND

○ What hazard or attack frightens you the most right now? Why is it particularly frightening?

○ What difference does it make for you to know that the Lord is on your side in this situation?

PRAY

Admit your fears to the Lord, and ask him for his peace as you trust him for deliverance. Thank God for the stories of deliverance in the Scriptures, in others' lives, and in your own life. Put your present and future in his hands.

---

*L. E. Toombs, "Traps and Snares," in *The Interpreter's Dictionary of the Bible*, ed. George Arthur Buttrick (Nashville: Abingdon, 1962), 688.

HAZARDOUS WORK

Every day I put faith on the line. I have never seen God. In a world where nearly everything can be weighed, explained, quantified, subjected to psychological analysis and scientific control, I persist in making the center of my life a God whom no eye hath seen, nor ear heard, whose will no one can probe. That's a risk.

Every day I put hope on the line. I don't know one thing about the future. I don't know what the next hour will hold. There may be sickness, accident, personal or world catastrophe. Before this day is over I may have to deal with death, pain, loss, rejection. I don't know what the future holds for me, for those I love, for my nation, for this world. Still, despite my ignorance and surrounded by tinny optimists and cowardly pessimists, I say that God will accomplish his will, and I cheerfully persist in living in the hope that nothing will separate me from Christ's love.

Every day I put love on the line. There is nothing I am less good at than love. I am far better in competition than in love. I am far better at responding to my instincts and ambitions to get ahead and make my mark than I am at figuring out how to love another. I am schooled and trained in acquisitive skills, in getting my own way. And yet I decide, every day, to set aside what I can do best and attempt what I do very clumsily—open myself to the frustrations and failures of loving, daring to believe that failing in love is better than succeeding in pride.

All that is hazardous work; I live on the edge of defeat all the time. I have never done any one of those things to my (or anyone else's) satisfaction. I live in the dragon's maw and at the flood's edge.

Psalm 124, though, is not about hazards but about help. The hazardous work of discipleship is not the subject of the psalm but only its setting. The subject is help: "Oh, blessed be GOD! . . . He didn't abandon us defenseless, helpless as a rabbit in a pack of snarling dogs. We've flown free from their fangs, free of their traps, . . . we're free as a bird in flight. GOD's strong name is our help, the same GOD who made heaven and earth" (*The Message*). Hazards or no hazards, the fundamental reality we live with is God who is *for us*; "GOD's strong name is our help."

When we are first in danger, our consciousness of hazard is total, like a bird trapped in a snare. All the facts add up to doom. There is no way out. And then, unaccountably, there *is* a way out. The snare breaks and the bird escapes. Deliverance is a surprise. Rescue is a miracle. "Oh, blessed be GOD! . . . He didn't abandon us defenseless."

How God wants us to sing like this! Christians are not fussy moralists who cluck their tongues over a world going to hell; Christians are people who praise the God who is on our side. Christians are not pious pretenders in the midst of a decadent culture; Christians are robust witnesses to the God who is our help. Christians are not fatigued outcasts who carry righteousness as a burden in a world where the wicked flourish; Christians are people who sing, "Oh, blessed be GOD! . . . He didn't abandon us defenseless." (Adapted from *A Long Obedience in the Same Direction*, 70-71)

JOY

PSALM 126

I know there are so-called Christians who never crack a smile and who can't abide a joke. But I don't meet very many of them. The stereotype of the somber Christian is a lie presumably created by the devil. One of the delightful discoveries along the way of Christian discipleship is how much enjoyment there is, how much laughter you hear, how much sheer fun you find.

Joy is characteristic of the Christian pilgrimage. It is the second in Paul's list of the fruits of the Spirit (Galatians 5:22). It is the first of Jesus' signs in the Gospel of John—turning water into wine.

Joy is not what we have to acquire in order to experience life in Christ; it is what comes to us when we are walking in the way of faith and obedience. We come to God (and to the revelation of God's ways) because none of us has it within ourselves, except momentarily, to be joyous. Joy cannot be commanded, purchased, or arranged. But we can decide to live in response to the abundance of God and not under the dictatorship of our own needs. One of the certain consequences of such a life is the kind of joy expressed in Psalm 126.

SESSION GOAL	READ
Rejoice in what God has done, is doing, and will do for us.	Chapters seven and eight of *A Long Obedience in the Same Direction*

REFLECT

○ How do you recognize a joyful person?

○ For you, what is the most joyful part of being a Christian?

STUDY

READ PSALM 126.

¹When the LORD restored the fortunes of Zion,
    we were like those who dreamed.
²Our mouths were filled with laughter,
    our tongues with songs of joy.
Then it was said among the nations,
    "The LORD has done great things for them."
³The LORD has done great things for us,
    and we are filled with joy.
⁴Restore our fortunes, LORD,
    like streams in the Negev.

⁵Those who sow with tears
   will reap with songs of joy.
⁶Those who go out weeping,
   carrying seed to sow,
will return with songs of joy,
   carrying sheaves with them.

The Babylonian king Nebuchadnezzar besieged Jerusalem for years and eventually conquered it in 586 BC. The city and temple were broken down and ransacked, many of the Jews were killed, and most of the survivors were taken into exile in Babylon. (See 2 Kings 24–25 and 2 Chronicles 36.) After the Persians took over the kingdom of the Babylonians, King Cyrus allowed the Jews to return and rebuild their city and temple (as related in Nehemiah and Ezra). Psalm 126 celebrates the return of the exiles from the Babylonian captivity.

1. When they finally returned from captivity, how did God's people react?

2. Imagine the scene: crowds of Jewish exiles returning from distant, pagan Babylon to their home city of Jerusalem. What do you see and hear?

> The central sentence in the psalm is "we are filled with joy" (v. 3). The words on one side of that center (vv. 1-2) are in the past tense, while the words on the other side (vv. 4-6) are in the future tense. Present gladness is not a happy result of good circumstances right now. Present gladness has both a past and a future.

3. How did their joy strengthen the Lord's reputation among the Gentiles?

4. When has someone's joy in the Lord's work been an encouragement to you to keep going?

5. For the psalmist, the return to Zion is a glorious memory in a time of current trouble (vv. 1-4). How do good memories increase your joy even in sorrowful times?

6. What promises does the psalm conclude with?

The Negev is the long southern triangle of modern
Israel, still known by that name today. Its watercourses
would be dry much of the year and then flood with
seasonal rain. Farmers carried their seed out to the
field and scattered it by hand, a laborious process.

7. Weeping while sowing seed for the future is a powerful image
of persevering in tough times. What "seeds" can you sow even
in sorrow or dryness?

RESPOND

○ Reflect on times you have been able to say with the psalmist,
"The LORD has done great things for us, and we are filled with
joy." How can you keep those times fresher in your memory?

○ In the light of past joys, we can continue to trust God even in
dry times. How will you express your joyful trust in him today?

PRAY

Express your joy in the Lord in some verbal or tangible way. Trust him that, no matter what happens, joy lies ahead for you.

PATIENCE

PSALM 129

S tick-to-it-iveness is one of the more inelegant words in the language, but I have a special fondness for it. I heard the word a great deal when I was young, mostly from my mother. I was a creature of sudden but short-lived enthusiasms. I had a passion for building model airplanes; and then one day, mysteriously, all desire left, and the basement was littered with half-finished models. Then stamp collecting became my all-consuming hobby. I received an immense stamp album for Christmas, joined a philatelic club, acquired piles and piles of stamps; and then one day, unaccountably, the interest left me. The album gathered dust, and the mounds of stamps were left unmounted. Next it was horses. Each Saturday morning my best friend and I would ride our bikes to a dude ranch two miles from town, get horses, and ride up into the Montana foothills, imagining we were Meriwether Lewis and William Clark, or, less pretentiously, Gene Autry and the Lone Ranger. And then, overnight, that entire world vanished and in its place was—girls.

Years later I learned that the church had a fancier word for what my mother meant: *perseverance*. I have also found that perseverance and patience are marks of Christian discipleship and have learned to admire those who exemplify them. Along the way Psalm 129 has gotten included in my admiration.

SESSION GOAL
See patience not as passivity but as
a force for good, and learn to wait
patiently for the Lord.

READ
Chapters nine through eleven of
*A Long Obedience in the Same
Direction*

REFLECT

◯ How easy is it for you to be patient?

◯ Who is the most patient person you know? Describe some
evidence of that person's patience.

STUDY

READ PSALM 129.

¹"They have greatly oppressed me from my youth,"
    let Israel say;
²"they have greatly oppressed me from my youth,
    but they have not gained the victory over me.
³Plowmen have plowed my back
    and made their furrows long.
⁴But the LORD is righteous;
    he has cut me free from the cords of the wicked."
⁵May all who hate Zion
    be turned back in shame.

⁶May they be like grass on the roof,
    which withers before it can grow;
⁷a reaper cannot fill his hands with it,
    nor one who gathers fill his arms.
⁸May those who pass by not say to them,
    "The blessing of the LORD be on you;
    we bless you in the name of the LORD."

1. As the psalmist looks back on his nation's history, what consistent pattern does he see?

Note in verses 3-4 that the harness cords connecting plow to oxen have been severed. The plows of persecution aren't working, and the plowmen haven't even noticed! They plod back and forth, unaware that their opposition is worthless. If they ever looked behind them (which they never do—their stiff necks make that exercise too painful), they would see that their bluster and blasphemy are having no results at all.

2. Why has God intervened in attacks on Israel?

3. If you had written this psalm, who or what would "they" be in verses 1-2?

4. There is no sign in this psalm that Israel did anything to be delivered—except wait. What would you say that waiting teaches the psalmist about himself?

> Verses 1-3 describe the psalmist's suffering. He has discovered his own endurance in the midst of oppression, as his enemies have not been victorious over him.

5. What does waiting teach the psalmist about God?

6. What has waiting taught you about God?

7. What is the writer's wish for the destiny of God's enemies (vv. 5-8)?

Palestinian houses were flat topped, and dirt was spread on the roofs for insulation. Seeds would sprout and grow from this dirt, but the grass didn't last; the thin soil couldn't support it. By midday the grass withered. No harvest there. The illustration is a cartoon, designed to bring a smile to the people of faith. The life of the world that is opposed or indifferent to God is barren and futile.

8. How does the writer express patience even in his wish for the destiny of God's enemies?

RESPOND

○ When has the Lord enabled you to remain patient under attack?

○ What are some long-term "oppressions" in your life in which you need patience for victory (as in vv. 1-2)?

PRAY

Remember that patience is never enjoyable at the moment. Thank God for past and future victories, and ask him for the continual grace of patience.

HOPE

PSALM 130

I was once a watchman. I worked from 10 p.m. until 6 a.m. in a building in New York City. My work as a night watchman was combined with that of elevator operator, but the elevator work petered out about midnight. After that I sat and read, dozed, or studied.

There were assorted night people in the neighborhood who would stop in and visit with me: strange, bizarre people with wonderful stories. I will never know how much of what I heard from them was fact and how much was fiction: a failed millionaire obsessed with communist plots responsible for his demise, a South American adventurer now too old to tramp the remote jungles and mountains, a couple of streetwalkers who on slow nights would sit and talk about God and the worth of their souls.

The people who employed me thought it was worth several dollars an hour for me to wait through the night and watch for the morning. But I never did anything, never constructed anything, never made anything happen. I waited.

If I had not known that there were others in charge of the building, I might not have been content to just be a watchman and collect my pay. If I were not confident that the building had an owner who cared about it, if I did not know that there was a building engineer who kept it in good order and repair, if I did not know that there were hundreds of people in the building who were going about their work every day quite capably . . . if I had not known these things, I might not have been so relaxed in making idle gossip with women of the night and old men of storied pasts.

Nor would the psalmist have been content to be a watchman if he were not sure of God. The psalmist's and the Christian's waiting and hoping are based on the conviction that God is actively involved in his creation and vigorously at work in redemption.

SESSION GOAL	READ
Focus on God as our great hope.	Chapters twelve and thirteen of *A Long Obedience in the Same Direction*

REFLECT

◉ Think back to a time when the Lord fulfilled your hopes. How did the experience strengthen your relationship with him?

◉ How did the actual events compare to your expectations of how and when your hopes would be fulfilled?

READ PSALM 130.

¹Out of the depths I cry to you, LORD;
  ²Lord, hear my voice.
Let your ears be attentive
  to my cry for mercy.
³If you, LORD, kept a record of sins,
  Lord, who could stand?
⁴But with you there is forgiveness,
  so that we can, with reverence, serve you.
⁵I wait for the LORD, my whole being waits,
  and in his word I put my hope.
⁶I wait for the Lord
  more than watchmen wait for the morning,
  more than watchmen wait for the morning.
⁷Israel, put your hope in the LORD,
  for with the LORD is unfailing love
  and with him is full redemption.
⁸He himself will redeem Israel
  from all their sins.

1. What insight does this passage give to the psalmist's relationship to the Lord?

2. The psalmist is obviously in deep trouble or distress of some kind. What keeps his situation from being hopeless?

3. How does God's mercy inspire hope (vv. 3-4, 7)?

> Note how each verse of the psalm includes a positive
> statement about the Lord. The mercy of God spells
> hope for us only after we have realized that our
> situation without God's mercy is hopeless (v. 3).

4. What reasons does the writer give Israel for putting their hope in the Lord?

5. What are some false hopes that people have?

> There are many worldly hopes: unshakable financial
> security, health and fitness into old age, status, longevity,
> power in relationships. These things bring benefits, but
> they are not guaranteed to be there when we need them.

6. Throughout this psalm, the character of God inspires the psalmist's hope. What is it about God's character that maintains your hope?

Note that eight times the name of God is used in this psalm. As we observe how God is addressed, we find that he is understood as one who forgives sin, who comes to those who wait and hope in him, who is characterized by steadfast love and plenteous redemption, and who will redeem Israel. God makes a difference. He acts positively toward his people.

7. For what are you waiting and watching in your spiritual life?

RESPOND

- In what "depths" do you now find yourself, perhaps as a result of your experience of waiting?

- How might worldly hopes be holding you in the depths?

- What part can God's forgiveness play in reaching into those depths?

PRAY

Praise God for being Lord of your future. Ask him to cleanse you of false worldly hopes and help you rest your hope solely in him.

FAITH

PSALM 132

The most religious places in the world are not churches but battlefields and mental hospitals. You are much more likely to find passionate prayer in a foxhole than in a church pew, and you will probably find more otherworldly visions and supernatural voices in a mental hospital than you will find in a church.

Nevertheless, we Christians don't go to either place to nurture our faith. We don't deliberately put ourselves in places of fearful danger to evoke heartfelt prayer, and we don't put ourselves in psychiatric wards to be around those who see visions of heaven and hell and hear the voice of God. What most Christians do is come to church, a place that is fairly safe and moderately predictable. We have an instinct for health and order in our faith.

But in doing that we don't get what some people seem to want very much: a religion that makes us safe at all costs, certifying us as inoffensive to our neighbors and guaranteeing us as good credit risks to the banks. It would be simply awful to find that as we grew in Christ we became dull, that as we developed in discipleship we became like Anthony Trollope's Miss Thorne, whose "virtues were too numerous to describe, and not sufficiently interesting to deserve description" (*Barchester Towers*).

We want a Christian faith that has stability but is not petrified, that has vision but is not hallucinatory. How do we get both the sense of stability and the spirit of adventure, the ballast of good health and the zest of true sanity? How do we get the adult maturity to keep our feet on the ground and retain the childlike innocence to make the leap of faith? Psalm 132 shows obedience as a lively, adventurous response of faith rooted in historical fact and reaching into a promised hope.

SESSION GOALS	READ
Become more sensitive to areas where we should deepen our faith in and obedience to God.	Chapters fourteen through sixteen of *A Long Obedience in the Same Direction*

REFLECT

○ If you were to rate the purposes that drive your life, where on the list would faith in the Lord come?

○ When is your faith in God most real for you?

STUDY

READ PSALM 132.

¹LORD, remember David
    and all his self-denial.
²He swore an oath to the LORD,
    he made a vow to the Mighty One of Jacob:

³"I will not enter my house
  or go to my bed,
⁴I will allow no sleep to my eyes
  or slumber to my eyelids,
⁵till I find a place for the Lᴏʀᴅ,
  a dwelling for the Mighty One of Jacob."
⁶We heard it in Ephrathah,
  we came upon it in the fields of Jaar:
⁷"Let us go to his dwelling place,
  let us worship at his footstool, saying,
⁸'Arise, Lᴏʀᴅ, and come to your resting place,
  you and the ark of your might.
⁹May your priests be clothed with your righteousness;
  may your faithful people sing for joy.'"
¹⁰For the sake of your servant David,
  do not reject your anointed one.
¹¹The Lᴏʀᴅ swore an oath to David,
  a sure oath he will not revoke:
"One of your own descendants
  I will place on your throne.
¹²If your sons keep my covenant
  and the statutes I teach them,
then their sons will sit
  on your throne for ever and ever."
¹³For the Lᴏʀᴅ has chosen Zion,
  he has desired it for his dwelling, saying,
¹⁴"This is my resting place for ever and ever;
  here I will sit enthroned, for I have desired it.
¹⁵I will bless her with abundant provisions;
  her poor I will satisfy with food.
¹⁶I will clothe her priests with salvation,

and her faithful people will ever sing for joy.

¹⁷"Here I will make a horn grow for David
   and set up a lamp for my anointed one.

¹⁸I will clothe his enemies with shame,
   but his head will be adorned with a radiant crown."

1. What words and phrases indicate how David feels about God?

2. What consuming purpose is David pursuing (vv. 2-5)?

3. What was the mood when the ark of the covenant was finally brought to Jerusalem (vv. 7-9)?

Years earlier, the Philistines had captured the ark of the covenant. When David became king he defeated the Philistines. Then one of his first royal acts was to go get the ark from where it was being kept. He brought the ark up to Jerusalem in festive parade, as portrayed in this psalm. While the song was sung, "David was dancing before the LORD with all his might, while he and all Israel were bringing up the ark of the LORD with shouts and the sound of trumpets" (2 Samuel 6:14-15).

4. This passage gives us a sense of David's joy in persistently following God. What keeps you persisting in your faith?

We should not be intimidated by David in this passage. David's own story includes many ups and downs in following God. Still, we see here that the times of strong obedience brought him great joy.

5. How did the Lord assure Israel of future blessings (vv. 11-18)?

6. How does the faithfulness of others (past or present) inspire you to persevere in obeying God?

To gain inspiration from the faithfulness of others, think of specific people whose obedience to the Lord has been an example to you. You might include biblical people, well-known Christians, unsung heroes you have heard of, personal acquaintances, or family members.

7. How does the assurance of God's faithfulness encourage you to obey him?

8. How would you describe the relationship between faith and obedience?

RESPOND

○ Obedience to God can be strengthened in any area: where we are now actively disobeying, where we are now just indifferent, or where we are now obeying God halfheartedly or only outwardly. Where would you like to strengthen your obedience to the Lord?

○ How will you bring those parts of your life into closer harmony with God's will?

PRAY

Thank God for the rewards and blessings that have come into your life through believing and obeying him. Thank him also for the people whose obedience serves as a living example for you. Confess any disobedience, and commit yourself to following him.

LEADING A
SMALL GROUP

L eading a Bible discussion can be an enjoyable and rewarding experience. But it can also be intimidating—especially if you've never done it before. If this is how you feel, you're in good company.

Remember when God asked Moses to lead the Israelites out of Egypt? Moses replied, "Please send someone else" (Exodus 4:13)! But God gave Moses the help (human and divine) he needed to be a strong leader.

Leading a Bible discussion is not difficult if you follow certain guidelines. You don't need to be an expert on the Bible or a trained teacher. The suggestions listed below can help you to effectively fulfill your role as leader—and enjoy doing it.

PREPARING FOR THE STUDY

1. As you study the passage before the group meeting, ask God to help you understand it and apply it in your own life. Unless this happens, you will not be prepared to lead others. Pray too for the various members of the group. Ask God to open your hearts to the message of his Word and motivate you to action.

2. Read the introduction to the entire guide to get an overview of the subject at hand and the issues that will be explored.

3. Be ready to respond to the "Reflect" questions with a personal story or example. The group will be only as vulnerable and open as its leader.

4. Read the chapter of the companion book that is recommended at the beginning of the session.

5. Read and reread the assigned Bible passage to familiarize yourself with it. You may want to look up the passage in a Bible so that you can see its context.

6. This study guide is based on the New International Version of the Bible. It will help you and the group if you use this translation as the basis for your study and discussion.

7. Carefully work through each question in the study. Spend time in meditation and reflection as you consider how to respond.

8. Write your thoughts and responses in the space provided in the study guide. This will help you to express your understanding of the passage clearly.

9. It might help you to have a Bible dictionary handy. Use it to look up any unfamiliar words, names, or places.

10. Take the final (application) study questions and the "Respond" portion of each study seriously. Consider what this means for your life, what changes you may need to make in your lifestyle, or what actions you can take in your church or with people you know. Remember that the group will follow your lead in responding to the studies.

LEADING THE STUDY

1. Be sure everyone in your group has a study guide and a Bible. Encourage the group to prepare beforehand for each discussion by reading the introduction to the guide and by working through the questions for that session.

2. At the beginning of your first time together, explain that these studies are meant to be discussions, not lectures. Encourage the members of the group to participate. However, do not put pressure on those who may be hesitant to speak during the first few sessions.

3. Begin the study on time. Open with prayer, asking God to help the group understand and apply the passage.

4. Have a group member read aloud the introductory paragraph at the beginning of the discussion. This will remind the group of the topic of the study.

5. Discuss the "Reflect" questions before reading the Bible passage. These kinds of opening questions are important for several reasons. First, there is usually a stiffness that needs to be overcome before people will begin to talk openly. A good question will break the ice.

   Second, most people will have lots of different things going on in their minds (dinner, an exam, an important meeting coming up, how to get the car fixed) that have nothing to do with the study. A creative question will get their attention and draw them into the discussion.

   Third, opening questions can reveal where our thoughts or feelings need to be transformed by Scripture. That is why it is important not to read the passage before the "Reflect" questions are asked. The passage will tend to color the honest reactions people would otherwise give, because they feel they are supposed to think the way the Bible does.

6. Have a group member read aloud the Scripture passage.

7. As you ask the questions, keep in mind that they are designed to be used just as they are written. You may simply read them aloud. Or you may prefer to express them in your own words.

   There may be times when it is appropriate to deviate from the study guide. For example, a question may already have been answered. If so, move on to the next question. Or someone may raise an important question not covered in the guide. Take time to discuss it, but try to keep the group from going off on tangents.

8. Avoid offering the first answer to a study question. Repeat or rephrase questions if necessary until they are clearly understood. An eager group quickly becomes passive and silent if members think the leader will give all the *right* answers.

9. Don't be afraid of silence. People may need time to think about the question before formulating their answers.

10. Don't be content with just one answer. Ask, "What do the rest of you think?" or, "Anything else?" until several people have given answers to a question. You might point out one of the study sidebars to help spur discussion; for example, "Does the quotation on page seventeen provide any insight as you think about this question?"

11. Acknowledge all contributions. Be affirming whenever possible. Never reject an answer. If it is clearly off-base, ask, "Which verse led you to that conclusion?" or, "What do the rest of you think?"

12. Don't expect every answer to be addressed to you, even though this will probably happen at first. As group members become

more at ease, they will begin to truly interact with each other. This is one sign of healthy discussion.

13. Don't be afraid of controversy. It can be stimulating! If you don't resolve an issue completely, don't be frustrated. Move on and keep it in mind for later. A subsequent study may solve the problem.

14. Try to periodically summarize what the group has said about the passage. This helps to draw together the various ideas mentioned and gives continuity to the study. But don't preach.

15. When you come to the application questions at the end of each "Study" section, be willing to keep the discussion going by describing how you have been affected by the study. It's important that we each apply the message of the passage to ourselves in a specific way.

    Depending on the makeup of your group and the length of time you've been together, you may or may not want to discuss the "Respond" section. If not, allow the group to read it and reflect on it silently. Encourage members to make specific commitments and to write them in their study guide. Ask them the following week how they did with their commitments.

16. Conclude your time together with conversational prayer. Ask for God's help in following through on the commitments you've made.

17. End the group discussion on time.

Many more suggestions and helps are found in The Big Book on Small Groups *by Jeffrey Arnold.*

SUGGESTED
RESOURCES

Steven Garber, *The Fabric of Faithfulness:*
Weaving Together Belief and Behavior

Elizabeth McQuoid, ed., *Persevere,*
Food for the Journey

J. A. Motyer, *The Message of Exodus:*
The Days of Our Pilgrimage

Trillia Newbell, *Sacred Endurance:*
Finding Grace and Strength for a Lasting Faith

Pete Sommer, *1 and 2 Timothy and Titus:*
Do What You Have Heard, LifeGuide Bible Studies

ALSO AVAILABLE

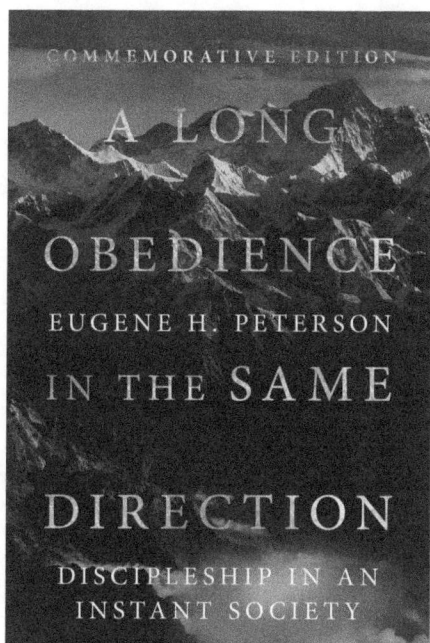

COMMEMORATIVE EDITION

A LONG

OBEDIENCE

EUGENE H. PETERSON

IN THE SAME

DIRECTION

DISCIPLESHIP IN AN
INSTANT SOCIETY

A Long Obedience in the Same Direction
Commemorative Edition
978-1-5140-1120-1